EAST
AIR

FINAL
FLIGHTLINE

EAST GERMAN AIR FORCE

FINAL FLIGHTLINE

C. J. van Gent

J. K. A. Bontje

Airlife
England

ACKNOWLEDGEMENTS

Acknowledgements go to Doctor Ottfried Franke, former Presse-Attaché of the 'DDR' in the Netherlands; Oberst Hempel and Oberstleutnant Franz-Lorenz Lill of the former Pressestelle der Luftstreitkräfte/Luftverteidigung der Deutschen Demokratischen Republik in Strausberg. Oberst Lill is now a member of the 'Presse und Öffentlichkeits–Arbeit' of the Kommando Luftstreitkräfte der Luftwaffe.

Special thanks go to Stefan Petersen, who proved to be not only an excellent Bundeswehr pilot, but also an observant photographer. He provided a number of air-to-air pictures of MiG–23s and MiG–29s. I wish to mention my wife Marijke who arranged many interviews during our photo-tour as well as my friend Jan Bontje who translated the texts. His wife Annemiek has also to be mentioned because her positive attitude to this project was a great help in its completion.

In addition I would like to mention Frank Elsinga who filled many a gap in my picture collection; Peter van Weenen, Kurt Thomsen, Martin Philips, Fred Willemse and Frans Scheve who allowed me to use their photos and slides. I am grateful to Fotag Berlin for their unique contribution. Last, but not least, I would like to mention Hendrik Jan van Broekhuizen and Harry Berger who made a farewell flight by helicopter and who spontaneously offered me some of their air-to-air pictures.

Furthermore, I wish to thank everyone else who has taken part in the creation of this book, in whatever way, including of course the people who so generously allowed me to visit the bases of the former LSK/NVA.

All pictures, unless stated otherwise: C. J. van Gent.

Printed in Singapore by Kyodo Printing PTE Ltd.

Airlife Publishing Ltd.
101 Longden Road, Shrewsbury SY3 9EB, England.

INTRODUCTION

The European political and military scene is changing faster than our imagination. New countries emerge and others disappear as if they were old actors in an absurd drama. One performer, East Germany, vanished from the stage completely. Even its architect and protector, the Soviet Union, foundered and gave (re-)birth to more than a dozen independent states.

This book is a flashback to a deceased airforce. The *Luftstreitkräfte/Luftverteidigung*, part of the *Nationale Volksarmee* of the German Democratic Republic, disappeared from the arena on 3 October, 1990, together with their employer.

Many of the depicted aircraft have already been destroyed. Others are now hardly more than rust and only a few were lucky enough to be sold. A few were placed in a museum. Only a few were taken over by the *Luftwaffe*; mainly transport aircraft and helicopters of the Mi–2 and Mi–8 type. The MiG–29 was the only fighter to be taken over – for a certain period. Some of the bases from which these aircraft operated were shut down and dismantled.

The *Nationale Volksarmee* was entirely ruled by the Soviets. As in all former Warsaw Pact countries, both matériel and organisation, including the flights, were entirely adapted to Soviet Airforce standards. Each base had fixed days (usually two) with fixed times, reserved for flights. The remaining days and hours were reserved for the Soviet Airforce. A *Flugtag* was always inaugurated with a so-called *Wetterflug* of a dual version of an aircraft type assigned to the base. Operational missions lacked fantasy. The pilots generally had to fly a fixed route for less than an hour. Then: back on the line, another pilot, refuel, and the next identical mission . . .

Though most bases were equipped with shelters, missions did not start straight from these shelters. The aircraft were towed to the flightline from which the missions took place. A remarkable aspect of the airbases was the variety of ground equipment needed before, during and after the flights. Most of it was mobile and could be repositioned quite easily.

Communication between pilot and airbase took place in Russian. The aftermath of the re-unification of both Germanies therefore resulted in a unique problem: none of the former East German aircraftmen spoke English. The communist training of the pilots was another problem. It was quite difficult to integrate pilots and ground personnel in the *Luftwaffe/Marineflieger*.

Furthermore both matériel and organisation of the former East German Airforce were, to Western standards, quite old-fashioned. The *Bundesrepublik* therefore was not too interested in integration with the leftovers of the East German Airforce.

Reason enough for the NVA to look at the unification with mixed feelings. For them the fusion was a confiscation. It felt as if only *they* had to make concessions. The number of personnel of the *Luftstreitkräfte* for example, 30,000 personnel, was immediately reduced to 4,000. The remainder became unemployed and feared the future: would they ever get another job? For many of them, the fast changes caused disorientation.

Though the GDR and its airforce only existed for a short period, they both made a great impression. The *Luftstreitkräfte* was founded in 1950 as a section of the East German *Volksleger*. Its nucleus was made up of two air defence divisions. These divisions were split up into *Geschwader* (wings) which in their turn were divided into two or three *Staffel* (squadrons). A *Staffel* normally included about twelve aircraft: usually ten singles and two dual–seaters.

In the West, standardization holds all the winning cards. In East Germany however, each *Staffel* had its own type. Even when the same type was used, different versions were employed, with considerable variations in operational and flight behaviour. Often, quantity overshadowed quality; the LSK possessed enormous numbers of MiG–21s in many versions, much more than was reasonably necessary. Though the newest version of this aircraft was greatly modified compared with the original type, it was, to our Western standards, completely outdated. Yet it was the backbone of the East German Airforce until its very last day. The MiG–23 too was used in several versions. Two *Geschwader* employed them. Another prominent aircraft was the Sukhoi Su–22M, also used by two *Geschwader*, both based at Laage. This base, the most modern in East Germany, was not completely ready until 1982, though it was in actual use since 1981. One of these *Geschwader*, MFG–28, served the *Marine* (Navy). The machines usually operated over the Baltic and specialized in maritime strike missions. The slightly more modern MiG–29 was used in small numbers only. An order for more machines was cancelled due to the re-unification. For transport, training and miscellaneous purposes, helicopters of the Mi–2 type were used, together with many versions of the Mi–8. Most commonly this Mi–8 was armed, usually being equipped with weapon racks on both sides of the fuselage. An exception was the Mi–8S (Salon) which was only used for the transportation of passengers. Apart from the passenger's cabin it also differed from other versions by its square windows.

At that time the very old Antonov An–2 was still in use. This museum piece was used for various tasks. The Zlinn Z–43, a single-engined four-seater similar to the Piper Cherokee class, was commonly used for liaison and courier services. For training and transport purposes two *Staffel* used the Let L–410 Turbolet. For heavy transports as well as passenger transportation both the Antonov An–26 and the Tupolev Tu–134 were employed. If necessary, aircraft like the Il–62, Tu–134 and Tu–154 of *Interflug*, the former civil airline of East Germany, were used.

The training of fighter pilots was the responsibility of *Geschwader 25*. It used the L–39 jet trainer. An adjusted version was used at Peenemünde as a target tug. After three or four years the instruction of the fighter pilots was taken over by *Geschwader 15*. This unit used several versions of the MiG–21, such as some of the older versions of the dual 21U and the single 21SPS. The conversion to the MiG–23 or Su–22 took place at the home base of that type.

The training of helicopter pilots took place on the Mi–2 and the Mi–8T. Transport pilots were trained on the An–2 and L–410 Turbolet.

The *Marine* possessed its own helicopter unit on Parow. *Marinehubschrauber – Geschwader 18* was equipped with three versions of the Mi–8 and two versions of the amphibious Mi–14. These aircraft were used for miscellaneous purposes.

The East German Army had its own *Armeefliegerkräfte* with two *Helikopter–Geschwader*, one at Basepohl and the other at Cottbus. The backbone of these *Geschwader* was the Mi–24D Hind. Both bases used also the Mi–2, the Mi–8 (in all different versions) and the Mi–9. The Mi–24P with a slightly heavier armour was used only at Basepohl. The Mi–9, in fact a modified Mi–8, was utilised as a mobile command base.

An Antonov An–26 over the late German Democratic Republic. (Photo: FOTAG Berlin)

ORGANIZATION OF THE LUFTSTREITKRÄFTE/LUFTVERTEIDIGUNG

1 Luftverteidigungsdivision

JG1	Jagdfliegergeschwader 1, 'Fritz Schmenkel'	3 Staffel MiG–21MF/US/USM	Holzdorf
JG3	Jagdfliegergeschwader 3, 'Wladimir Komarow'	2 Staffel MiG–29/MiG–29UB	Preschen
		1 Staffel MiG–21MF/US/USM	Preschen
JG8	Jagdfliegergeschwader 8, 'Hermann Matern'	2 Staffel MiG–21bis/bis/UM	Maxwalde
VFK/1	Verbindungsflugkette	2x An–2, 3x Z–43	Cottbus

3 Luftverteidigungsdivision

JG2	Jagdfliegergeschwader 2, 'Juri Gagarin'	3 Staffel MiG–21M/US/USM	Neubrandenburg
JG9	Jagdfliegergeschwader 9, 'Heinrich Rau'	1 Staffel MiG–23MF/UB	Peenemünde
		2 Staffel MiG–23ML	Peenemünde
FDK33	Flugzieldarstellungskette 33	2x L–39ZO, 3x L–39V	Peenemünde
VFK/3	Verbindungsflugkette	2x An–2, 3x Z–43	Neubrandenburg

Kommando der Front und Transportfliegerkrafte

VFS14	Verbingdungsfliegerstaffel	5x An–2, 4x Let L–410 UVP, 4x Z–43	Strausberg
TS24	Transportfliegerstaffel 24	1 Staffel An–26	Dresden
TFG44	Transportfliegergeschwader 44, 'Arthur Pieck'	Tu–134A, Mi–8S	Marxwalde
THG34	Transporthubschraubergeschwader 34 'Werner Seelenbinder'	2 Staffel Mi–8T/S	Brandenburg
MHG18	Marinehubschraubergeschwader 18	2 Staffel Mi–8T/BT/S, Mi–14BT/PL	Parow
MFG28	Marinefliegergeschwader 28, 'Paul Wieczorek'	2 Staffel Su–22M–4/Su–22M–3U	Laage
JBG37	Jagdbomberfliegergeschwader 37, 'Klement Gottwald'	2 Staffel MiG–23BN/UB	Drewitz
JBG77	Jagdbomberfliegergeschwader 77 'Gebhard Leberecht von Blücher'	2 Staffel Su–22M–4/Su–22M–3U	Laage
TAFS47	Taktische Aufklärung Fliegerstaffel 47	1 Staffel MiG–21M/U	Preschen
TAFS87	Taktische Aufklärung Fliegerstaffel 87	1 Staffel MiG–21M/U	Drewitz

Offiziershochschule der LSK/LV für Militärflieger 'Otto Lilienthal'   Bautzen

FAG15	Fliegerausbildungsgeschwader 15 'Heinz Kapelle'	2 Staffel MiG–21U/US/USM/SPS	Rothenburg
FAG25	Fliegerausbildungsgeschwader 25 'Leander Ratz'	2 Staffel L–39ZO	Rothenburg
HAG35	Hubschrauberausbildungsgeschwader 35	18x Mi–2, 18x Mi–8T/S	Brandenburg
TAS45	Transportfliegerausbildungsgeschwader 45	12x An–2, 8x Let L–410 UVP, 3x Z–43	Kamenz

Armeefliegerkräfte

KHG3	Kampfhubschraubergeschwader 3, 'Ferdinand von Schill'	1 Staffel Mi–24D	Cottbus
		1 Staffel Mi–8TB	Cottbus
HSFA3	Hubschrauberstaffel der Führung und Aufklärung 3	Mi–2S, Mi–8S, Mi–9	Cottbus
KHG5	Kampfhubschraubergeschwader 5 'Adolf von Lützow'	1 Staffel Mi–24D/P	Basepohl
HSFA5	Hubschrauberstaffel der Führung und Aufklärung 5	Mi–2S, Mi–8S, Mi–9	Basepohl

Offiziershochschule der LSK/LV 'Franz Mehring'   none   Kamenz
Militärtechnische Schule der LSK/LV 'Harry Kuhn'   none   Bad Düben

Note Transportfliegergeschwader 44 on Marxwalde was directly commanded by the LSK/LV. If necessary, Interflug aircraft of the type Tu–134, Tu–154 and Il–62 were used.

GLOSSARY

Armeefliegerkräfte	Army Air Command
Fliegerausbildungsgeschwader (FAG)	Fighter Training Wing
Flugzieldarstellungskette (FDK)	Target-Tug Flight
Hubschrauberausbildungsgeschwader (HAG)	Helicopter Training Wing
Hubschrauberstaffel der Führung und Aufklärung (HSFA)	Helicopter Squadron for Communication and Reconnaissance
Jagdbomberfliegergeschwader (JBG)	Fighter Bomber Wing
Jagdfliegergeschwader (JG)	Fighter Wing
Kampfhubschraubergeschwader (KHG)	Combat Helicopter Wing
Kommando der Front und Transportfliegerkräfte	Bomber and Transport Command
Luftverteidigungsdivision	Air Defense Division
Marinefliegergeschwader (MFG)	Marine Fighter Wing
Marinehubschraubergeschwader (MHG)	Marine Helicopter Wing
Militärtechnische Schule	Military Technical School
Offiziershochschule	Officers' College/Air Academy
Taktische Aufklärungfliegerstaffel (TAFS)	Tactical Reconnaissance Squadron
Transportfliegerstaffel (TS)	Transport Squadron
Transportfliegergeschwader (TFG)	Transport Wing
Transportfliegerausbildungsgeschwader (TAS)	Transport Training Wing
Transportfliegerausbildungstaffel	Transport Training Squadron
Transporthubschraubergeschwader (THG)	Transport Helicopter Wing
Verbindungflugkette (VFK)	Liaison Flight
Verbindungstaffel	Liaison Squadron

Antonov An-2

An Antonov An–2 of VFK–1 at Cottbus in preparation for a mission. This aircraft type was the only one to stay in service from the launching of the LSK in 1956 until the very last minute.

Left: Over an East German forest the camouflage of the Antonov An–2 (in this case of VFS–14) serves well.
(Photo: Kommando Luftstreitkräfte, Strausberg)

Below: An An–2 being relocated at Cottbus. This old workhorse was mainly used for light transport and liaison purposes.

Antonov An–26

Right: The most important transport aircraft of the NVA/LSK was the Antonov An–26. In total twelve of these machines were used by TS–24 at Dresden.

Below: The 'office' of the An–26 at work.

Below: Unlike the other An–26s, which were all painted in camouflage colours, the '384' was entirely light grey. (Photo: F. Elsinga)

Opposite: Close-up of the navigator's observation blister and the four-blade constant-speed fully-feathering propellers, driven by Ivchenko AI–24WT turboprop engines.

Let L–410 UVP Turbolet

Below: A rainy day, the left engine already started: this L–410 UVP of VFS 14 is almost ready for take-off from Strausberg Base.

Right: The beautiful highwing L–410 UVP is of Czechoslovakian origin. It was used by the LSK from 1981 onwards. This machine of VFS-14 at Strausberg was used for transportation.

Let L–39 Albatross

These steps made climbing into the cockpit easier.

Below: A total of forty Albatross L–39ZOs were used for training purposes. All of them were employed by FAG 25 at Rothenburg.

Opposite: One of two L–39V target tugs at Peenemünde. Both machines, the '170' and the '171', were used by FDK–33. The backseat was replaced by the winchdrum. A cable with a maximum length of 985ft (approx. 300m) was used to drag the 15ft (approx. 5m) long 'target' KT–04.

Below: Though not equipped with the towing system for tugging the KT–04, the L–39ZOs of FDK 33 were employed for several tasks. The backseat was not removed, as this taxying '187' demonstrates.

Right: The L–39ZO was also used as a light attack aircraft. Here is the '187' again, this time equipped with external tanks and rocketpods with unguided air-to-ground missiles.
(Photo: Fred Willemse)

Mikoyan MiG–15 UTI

Mikoyan MiG–17F

Opposite: Though no longer in active service, this MiG–15 UTI was used as an instructional airframe at Drewitz. In 1984 it was struck off charge as the very last one of its kind. (Photo: F. Elsinga)

Below: Like the preceding MiG–15, this machine was no longer in active service but was used as an instructional airframe at Drewitz. (Photo: F. Elsinga)

Mikoyan MiG–21

Right: The first MiG–21 version received by the LSK was the MiG 21F–13 (type 74). This type was no longer operational, but on most bases it could be seen as a decoy, as at Marxwalde.

Below: The MiG–21SPS (type 94) was the oldest version of the MiG–21 in use. It was mainly used for training purposes by FAG 15 at Rothenburg. Unlike the former type, the canopy opened sideways. It also had a much broader tail fin with a 'chute housing.

Below: This MiG–21US of TAFS 87 at Drewitz was returning from a mission and had just dropped its 'chute.

Right: Before camouflage came into use, most of the machines were painted pale aluminium like this MiG–21USM. (Photo: via M.J. Philips)

Below: A MiG–21M (type 88) of TAFS 47 at Preschen. Note the photo reconnaissance equipment under the inboard wingpylons. Outwardly it differed from the SPS by the broad spine of its fuselage.

Opposite: The MiG–21MF (type 96) differed from the 'M' version by a more powerful engine. Also, the canopy had a rearview mirror.

Left: Trailing its 'chute this MiG–21USM (type 69) of JG–3 arrives at Preschen. It is the dual version of the MiG–21M and usually it was called 'UM'.

Below: The 'chute is dropped and the '229' taxies to the flightline. The USM/UM differed from the MiG–21US by the antenna on its dorsal spine.

Below: MiG–21bis '936' taxying to the runway. In the background a wrapped Fishbed. Spread all over the various MiG–21 bases one could often see these covered machines.

Right: An engine-test of a MiG–21bis. This type was the most modern version of the MiG–21 family and the only real resemblance with its predecessors was in its appearance. In fact it was a total new design. The 'bis' was only used by JG–8 of Marxwalde.

Below: A 'bis' being towed from its shelter to the flightline. Note the remarkable form of the wing.

Right: Armed-to-the-teeth at Marxwalde. A 'bis' in standby position for a scramble start comparable with the Quick Reaction Alert (QRA).

Below: The weapons attached to the pylons under the wings are AA–2–2 'Advanced Atoll' (in former Soviet classification K–13) air-to-air missiles. One is IR-homing, the other radar-guided.

Opposite: Simple repairs could be done at the flightline, as shown here with the changing of a wheel of a 'bis' at Marxwalde. The machine is lifted from the ground with jacks.

Mikoyan MiG–23

Below: With an RBS under its wing this 'MF' waits for clearance to take off. Remarkable is the big stabilo which runs halfway along the fuselage, with the sharp nick.

Right: The MiG–23MF was the first version of this 'swing-wing' within the LSK and entered service in 1978. This type was used by JG–9 at Peenemünde where this picture was taken.

Below: Under the fuselage of this MiG–23 we see AA–8 'Aphid' IR-homing AAMs. Unlike the 'Apex' this is a close-range air-to-air weapon. (Photo: F. Elsinga)

Right: A start with afterburner on is always a fascinating sight. A MiG–23MF of JG–9 takes off from the runway of Peenemünde.

Below: The MiG–23UB dual was used by both JG–9 and JBG–37 at Drewitz. The one shown belonged to JBG–37. Note the odd and colourful camouflage.

Right: The MiG–23ML, also in service with JG–9 at Peenemünde, was of a much more modern kind than the 'MF'. The stabilo was much smaller and lacked the typical nick. Also, due to a changed landing gear the position of the fuselage was more horizontal.

Left: Critical weather at Drewitz: inbetween two showers this MiG–23UB (105) is on finals.

Below: Another MiG–23UB during take-off catching the last sunshine just before the storm breaks.

Below: At Drewitz JBG–37 used the MiG–23BN. Starting at the intakes the nose section of this fighter-bomber has been completely changed, thus making it in fact a transmute from MiG–23 to MiG–27.

Right: A MiG–23BN having problems with its landing gear.

Left: The ventral fin of the MiG–23 is connected with the landing gear. As soon as the wheels are retracted, the fin falls downwards into flight position. When preparing for landing and the wheels are unlocked the fin topples over to the right.

Below: A MiG–23BN just airborne. Though the landing gear has not yet been fully retracted the ventral fin is already in flight position.

Bottom: A MiG–23BN using its brake 'chute to reduce its landing run. This eight bar 'chute, though unusually large, was apparently very efficient.

Below and Opposite: MiG–23BNs of JBG–37 at Drewitz in their element. The machines here still carry a four-digit serial. Later on the first digit was removed. (Photo: via M.J. Philips)

(Photo: Stefan Petersen)

(Photo: Stefan Petersen)

Below: A MiG–23ML of JG–9 accelerating with full afterburner. (Photo: Stefan Petersen)

Opposite: A MiG–23ML over colourful cloud-cover. (Photo: Stefan Petersen)

Right: MiG–23ML '569' passing the Baltic coast-
line of Eastern Germany. (Photo: Stefan Petersen)

Below: '569' again in her element. Notice the
giant central fin which was flipped over
during the landing. (Photo: Stefan Petersen)

Below: During the dismissal of the NVA, JG–9 made its farewell in a proper way with this MiG–23ML '488'. Afterwards this machine still wore this outfit with the *Bundeswehr* serial 20+26.

Right: The 'swing-wing' concept of the MiG–23 is clearly visible here, with the wings fully spread. (Photo: Stefan Petersen)

Mikoyan MiG–29

A MiG–29 of JG–3 on finals at Preschen. The LSK possessed twenty of these modern fighters. A new order was cancelled because the NVA was dismissed.

Left: A MiG–29 and a MiG–29UB in a break over Preschen.

Below: Touch-down of a MiG–29 at Preschen. Note the smoking rubber.

Below: A MiG–29 using its brake 'chute.

Opposite: Once again a MiG–29 with 'chute. Note that the 'chute differs from that of the previous MiG. It was most probably borrowed from a MiG–21.

Below: Mission completed: The pilot leaves his MiG–29 and hands it over to the ground crew.

Right: A MiG–29 clearly showing its nozzles.

Below: Though the MiG–29 is one of the most modern fighters it has a conventional cockpit.

Right: The end of an operational day. The flightline is cleared and the aircraft are towed to their shelters.

Below: A beautiful contrast, this MiG–29 in front of the edge of a peaceful wood.
(Photo: F. Elsinga)

Right: The MiG–29UB was the dual version of the MiG–29. Only four of them have been used. The air intake louvres above the intakes can be locked. On the ground they take over the function of the latter to avoid FOD (Foreign Object Damage).

Below: A MiG–29 of JG–3 over closed cloud-cover. (Photo: Stefan Petersen)

Opposite: The nose section in close-up. (Photo: Stefan Petersen)

Below: Two MiG–29s dog fighting.
(Photo: Kommando Luftstreitkräfte, Strausberg)

Right: In close formation the splendid contours of the MiG–29 seen at their best.
(Photo: FOTAG Berlin)

Left: The forests of the GDR proving the effectiveness of MiG–29 camouflage.
(Photo: Stefan Petersen)

Below: After the re-unification this MiG–29 was newly-registered as 29+01 and served with the *Bundeswehr*. For quite a long period it remained with this special outfit.

Bottom: These colours of the '604' were the parting gift of JG–3 just before the curtain fell for both this *Geschwader* and the whole NVA, on 27 September, 1990.

Mil Mi–2

The Isotov GTD–350 turbines were compact indeed. The Mi–2 had one of them on each side.

Below: This Mi–2S was used by HSFA 3 at Cottbus and therefore served with the *Armeefliegerkräfte*. It was equipped with an additional external fuel tank.

Right: The letters SMH mean *Schnelle Medizinische Hilfe*, 'Quick Medical Aid'.

Mil Mi–8

A busy day at Brandenburg. One helicopter awaiting clearance for take-off while another one arrives. The Mi–8T was the principal helicopter of the LSK and was used from 1968 onwards.

Below: The Mi–8TB differed from the Mi–8T by virtue of its much heavier armour. The weapon racks consisted of three suspension-points plus three rocket-launchers. In the nose a flexible mounted 12.7mm machine gun. The picture shows a Mi–8TB of KHG–3 at Cottbus.

Opposite: The Mi–8T could be armed on both sides of the fuselage. Usually it carried UB–16 launchers each with sixteen S–5 57mm air-to-ground missiles.

Left: The cockpit section of a SAR Mi–8T. Note the open sash-window and the first aid box together with the rescue hoist right above the doorway.

Below: The Mi–8S (Salon) was a comfortable passenger version for eleven persons. Note the square windows. The machine shown here was of HSFA–3 at Cottbus.

Below: *Marinehubschraubergeschwader* MHG–18 at Parow also had one Mi–8S.

Right: A Mi–8TB of KHG–5 of Basepohl in its element. Note the UB–32 rocket-launchers. (Photo: F. Elsinga)

Below: The weapon rack of a Mi–8TB with a UB–32 rocket-launcher for thirty-two S–5 57mm air-to-ground missiles. Above the suspension points are launchers with AT–2 anti-tank rockets. (Photo: F. Elsinga)

Opposite: Two Mi–8TBs of KHG–5 at Basepohl during one of their last missions prior to the re-unification. (Photo: H.J. van Broekhuizen)

Below: MHG–18 also used a few Mi–8T helicopters for Search and Rescue (SAR).

Right: This Mi–8TB of MHG–18 may look different, but in every other way it was identical to the rest of the machines of the *Armeefliegerkräfte*.

Mil Mi–9

The Mi–9 looked like a Mi–8 with more antennae. These machines served with the *Armeefliegerkräfte* and were used as mobile HQs from Cottbus and Basepohl. This one belonged to HSFA–3 at Cottbus.

Mil Mi–14

Right: A Mi–14BT with a Mi–14PL on the background. The DISS 15 Doppler navigation system is placed in a box below the serial under the tail boom. The NATO Sea King was its counterpart.

Below: The complete crew of a Mi–14BT included a diver-frogman for rescue tasks over the Baltic. (Photo: F. Elsinga)

Below: The Mi–14PL also served with MHG–18 and was the anti-submarine version. It differed from the 'BT' because it lacked the bulge at the right just above the windows and the rear fuselage in which the MAD equipment can be seen.

Opposite: The Mi–14BT was not exactly Miss Universe... Note the front twin wheel-legs which retract forward and the large 'search' radar in front of the boat hull.

Mil Mi–24

A taxying Mi–24 of KHG–3 on the platform of Cottbus.

Below: All former Warsaw Pact countries used the Mi–24 gunship, including KHG–3 and KHG–5 of the *Armeefliegerkräfte*. They operated from Cottbus and Basepohl respectively. This machine of KHG–5 is training at Basepohl. (Photo: F. Elsinga)

Opposite: The auxiliary wing of a Mi–24 with, under the inboard pylon, a UB–32A rocketpod for thirty-two unguided air-to-ground 57mm S–5 missiles. Below the pylons one can just see the chaff and flare dispensers under the tail boom.

Below: A Mi–24D of KHG–5 over a forest in Eastern Germany. (Photo: H.J. van Broekhuizen)

Right: Until just before the re-unification of the two Germanies it was not known that KHG–5 at Basepohl used the Mi-24P, the most modern version of the Mi–24. Characteristic were the two 30mm cannons on the right side of the machine. (Photo: Kurt Thomsen)

Sukhoi Su–22M

This 'Fitter' leaves the flightline, towed by an APPA–5 aircraft-servicing vehicle bringing it to its shelter.

Overleaf: In the mid-eighties the LSK got the disposal of two *Geschwader* Su–22M fighter-bombers, both the 'single' and the 'dual' versions. Here we see a Su–22UM–3K (dual) and a Su–22m–4 (single) of JBG–77 in front of the maintenance hangar at Laage.

Below: A clean Su–22M–3K of JBG–77 on the platform at Laage.

Opposite: The Su–22M–4 of MFG–28 differed from the machines of JBG–77 by virtue of its twin chaff and flare dispensers.

Left: With unfolded 'chute this 'dual' returns from a mission.

Below: Both MFG–28 and JBG–77 of Laage said farewell in an appropriate manner. This Su–22M–4 belonged to JBG–77.

Tupolev Tu–134

Though TFG–44 at Marxwalde often used aircraft of Interflug, it possessed its own Tupolev Tu–134A with serial 184.

Zlin Z–43

The four-seat Zlin Z–43 was mainly used as a liaison-and-courier aircraft. The one shown was used by VFK–1 at Cottbus.

A glimpse of the ground equipment

A MiG–29 parked in a hardened aircraft shelter at Preschen. The shelters of all bases were built according to a specific pattern.

Below: Often the searchlights of three or four ZIL–159 vehicles served as landing lights.

Opposite: The TATRA T815 was used at Preschen to refuel the MiG–29.

Former LSK aircraft serving as Instructional Airframes at the 'Offiziershochschule' at Bautzen

The Ilyushin Il–14 was used as a transport, passenger and even a photo-reconnaissance aircraft. The last one served until 1980. They were replaced by the Antonov An–26.

Below: In 1959 a tug unit was formed, equipped with a number of Ilyushin Il–28 Beagles. Apart from the standard version of the Il–28 the LSK possessed two Il–28R and one Il–28U. The one displayed was struck off charge as the very last Beagle and flew to Bautzen on 20 October, 1982.

Right: The Antonov An–14 was built to succeed the An–2 but was in fact outlived by the latter. This was also the case within the LSK where this aeroplane was replaced by the L–410 Turbolet.

Below: Along with the MiG–17F the 'PF' was also used. While the 'F' version operated as a fighter-bomber, the 'PF' was an interceptor. The latter is recognizable from the radar antennae in and on the nose.

Opposite: The tail turret of an Il–28.

In 1962 the Let L–29 Delfin started service as basic trainer for the LSK as a successor to the MiG–15U. From 1978 onwards this machine was replaced by the L–39 Albatross from the same manufacturer.